A Best Friend Is Forever And Always

by MARTHA POPSON

The C.R. Gibson Company
Norwalk, Connecticut 06856

We got to know each other
so fast,
had so much in common,
how could we not
have found each other?

We were a friendship
looking for a place
to happen.

Meeting you was like
looking in the mirror
and, at last,
seeing a reflection—
or finding out
my language
wasn't so foreign
after all.

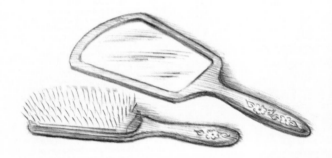

Do you remember
the day my hair
was sticking out funny
and everybody else said,
"Oh, it looks fine."
but you said, "No, it doesn't."
and helped me fix it?

You told the truth.

That showed you really cared.

I like it when
I see a cartoon
that'll make
you laugh and
I clip it out

or the phone rings
and it's you saying,
"Quick, turn on the
TV to channel 5."

Life goes better
with friends.

It's the little things
we do:
people watching at the mall,
spending a summer under the sun,
getting the giggles over nothing.

Knowing you is
just plain fun.

Whenever something
important happens,
I can tell my family
or my other friends—

but it doesn't
feel complete
until I tell you.

You and I—
we can talk about
almost anything
from silly games
("If you could choose,
what animal would you be?")
to serious stuff
("Will anybody ever love me
forever?")

We share the Silence, too.

Sometimes more gets said
without words
than in all our conversations.

When we reach
for the phone,
our parents say:
"What can you two
have to talk about—
you saw each other
in school all day."

Well, I can't
exactly make
a list,
but we never
run out of
things to say.

You know so much about me:
my dreams for the future,
what I worry about
just before I sleep,
what scares me most of all.

I wouldn't tell just anyone.

You've told me your secrets, too.

We trust each other.

You and I
spend hours
putting on
make-up
and
can't pass
a perfume counter
without trying
a scent or two.

We catch a glimpse
in the mirror
and wonder—
who are these
lovely creatures
we've created?

Not too long ago
we didn't care
if boys
noticed us
or not.

Now that's changed
and it's a delicious
confusion.

Aren't you glad
we're together
to sort it
all out?

We're definitely
yo-yos.

Our moods
go high
and low
with
awesome
speed.

Friendship's
never boring
with all these
ups
and
downs.

Sometimes I'm so happy that
I want to hug the whole world;
other days, I need to hold on
for dear life.

But people don't understand
if you get too close.

You do, don't you?

Sometimes I feel different from
everybody else on Earth.

I almost wonder if I'm an alien
from another planet dropped here
by mistake.

It's such a lonely feeling;
then I remember you
and how we are alike.

Did the spaceship stop twice?

If Ma Bell can reach out
and touch someone,
why can't we?

I found out just now
that he likes someone else.

You had tried to tell me
he was too old,
wouldn't even notice.

He didn't.

You didn't call it
puppy love or some
school-girl crush.

Pain is pain
whatever the age.

When you asked me to stay overnight
and I said not this time,
I needed to be alone,
you understood.

Friends don't always
have to say "yes".

When I say
how much I hurt
you listen.

You don't say,
"I know just
how you feel,"
unless you do
or ever, ever
laugh at me.

Sometimes, though,
when I am sad,
you say:
"You think that's bad?"
and tell something
so funny that
we end up in tears.

Some for pain,
some for joy.

Everyone
wants
to be needed.

You've needed me:
to help with homework,
to decide what to wear,
to listen when you were lonely.

It feels good
to know
I can help someone.

Remember that time
when
I was scared
and
you were scared
but
we were scared
together
and
it wasn't so bad?

Once in awhile
I get sick and
miss school.

I know you'll tell me:
what went on
who sat by whom
what they said at lunch
if anyone asked you
where I was.

You know what I want to hear.

It's not just what you
learned in history.

When something goes wrong
at school or home,
still I know I'm not alone:
I can call and you'll listen.

How does someone survive
without a friend to talk to?

The telephone is
my life line;
I'm so glad you're
on the other end.

It hurts so much
when friendship ends.
I had a friend once.
We used to be so close.
But then she had lessons
after school
and I had practice.
We didn't have much
to talk about anymore.
We still say "hi"
when we meet in the halls.

It was no one's fault really,
just one of those things.

I don't want that to ever
happen to us.

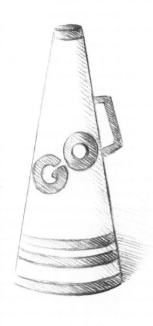

Usually
we get along
you and I.

But, now and then
I say something dumb
or you're in a grouchy mood.

It hurts when that happens,
but we can work it through.

Once my family stopped
to eat at this place—
lots of kids were there,
having fun with their friends.

One girl sat by herself,
acting like she didn't care
if she was alone.

But I remember how it feels
and how having just *one* friend
changes everything.

Life doesn't always
come out equal,
not even with friends.

Once
I had a date
and you came alone.

Once
you got an A
and I barely
made a C.

We're not the same,
but we're together.

We have so much
fun
just laughing
together.

It can start
with a smirk
or an
innocent grin.

Next it slips into
the giggles
or roars on to
the belly laughs.

If someone asks:
"What's so funny?"
There's no answer—
but if we look at
each other,
we start all over again.

We write
BFFAA
on the backs
of our letters.

That means
Best Friends
Forever and
Always.

There's no way
to guarantee it,
but we've made
a good start.

You and I
go together like
parts of a jigsaw puzzle.

Being friends with you
is like finding the piece
that was missing and
now is in place.

It fits just right.

Teachers never
give us the
right assignment.

If they asked,
"How do you
design a
friend?"

It'd be easy:

I'd draw a
picture of you.

Editorial direction by Jayne Bowman
Interior illustrations by Nancy Hannans
Designed by Patrice Barrett
Set in Souvenir Light